Angelique Kereecko

Heart of Passion
Designed and Written By
Angelique Kereecko

Angelique Kereecko

The blank page is my canvas.
My imagination is the paint brush.

-Angelique Kereecko

Angelique Kereecko

Table of Contents

Angelique Kereecko

Heart of Passion © 2023

Angelique Kereecko

Flow
Spiritual Love

Angelique Kereecko

Love Galaxy

I searched through every galaxy
I am closer to You
Try your best to meet me half way
Put your hand in mine
Finally You are here with me
Let our love flow
Put your trust in me
Let our love grow

In Love Emotionally
In Love Mentally
In Love Spiritually
In Love Harmony
In Love Deeply
In Love Truely
In Love Loyalty
In Love Religiously
In Love Honestly
In Love Definitely
In Love Infinity

Our love is our destiny
Our passion was written in the constellation
Please, tell me that you believe
We have met finally
We create our love galaxy
We inspire one another

Angelique Kereecko

Dancing In The Sky

It's a cryin' shame
You take me higher than cocaine
You take me beyond the Stars
You make me fly past Mars

Come away with me
Go higher with me
Ascend with me
A new paradise you see
You meet a Venus Star Angel
Once in a lifetime
It's your time to rise

I'm high on your love
I'm drunk on your love
I never want to come off of this
I never want to come down
Take flight above the sky
I can't come down, No, not now

Let your power take you high
I can not deny
I love to go high
This moment is the highlight of your life

Dancing in the sky
Morning, noon and night
Starting in July
Travel through Twilight
I can not deny
I love to go high
This is how I take flight

Angelique Kereecko

Better

Today is better than yesterday
Obstacles moved out my way
I'm living the best of my life
I got my good spell
I'm walking in my blessings

Dear Self, You deserve the very best
These blessings are on my life
I'm living in my blessings
I'm walking in my blessings

I see myself with a brighter future
You are doing well
You got good health
You got good wealth

Angelique Kereecko

Dear Sweet Heart

Dear sweet heart
No matter how many miles apart
There is always a special place
for you in my heart
Memories of your sweet face
Memories of your embrace
Memories can not be erased
No one can take your place

I see the light when I look into your eyes
I see the sunshine when I look at your face
You are a wonderful blessing
You are amazing
Knowing you is the best blessing

I been in love with you
Since the first day we met
The first day that we started
No more broken hearted

Angelique Kereecko

Congratulations

Congratulations on your graduation
Congratulations on your new career
Congratulations on your promotion
Congratulations on your new house
Congratulations on your new car
Congratulations starting your new business
Congratulations on your wedding
Congratulations on your new baby
Congratulations paying off debt
It feels good living debt free

I am happy to see you smile
I am happy to hear you laugh
I am happy for your progress
I am happy for your success
I am happy with you
I am happy for you
Congratulations on all the good things you achieve

Celebrate like it's New Years
Celebrate like it's your Birthday
Make today your own Holiday
Celebrate your own Holiday
I'm happy to see you winning
Congratulations on your new beginning

No jealousy
No time for jealousy
No envy

Angelique Kereecko

No time for envy
Not wasting energy on jealousy or envy
I'm happy to see you winning
Congratulations on your new beginning

I am proud to see you doing better
I am happy to see the new version of you
Healthy, Happy, Wealthy
I am proud of you
So, very proud of you

Angelique Kereecko

A Million Kisses All Over Again

A million kisses I give to you
I can never love you too much
A million wishes I grant to you
I can never cherish you too much
A million memories I share with you
I can never be with you too much
I love every word you speak
I do absolutely adore you
I listen to your heartbeat
Every moment is captivating
You speak softly
A million years from now
I would do this all over again
I have no regrets about us
I would relive all over again
You would have the same face
You would have the same name
We would be in the same place
A million years from now
I would choose you all over again
A million kisses I give to you
I can never love you too much
A million wishes I grant to you
I can never cherish you too much
A million memories I share with you
I can never be with you too much

Angelique Kereecko

Love Blessings

Anoint me with your love
Baptize me with your love
Bless me with your love
Convert me to your love

We do this all for love
Love Blessings
Love, Love, Love Blessings
Love, Love, Love Blessings

Your love is my blessing
Your love is my covenant
Your love is my salvation

Angelique Kereecko

Angelite, Part 1

Angelite shining bright
Showing truth through your eyes

Angelite, we have been waiting for your arrival
No need to be surprised
You bring the Keys to Life
You give the Keys to Life
Unlock the Treasures
The door is open for you
Walk into your blessings

Angelite, speaking to me
Angelite, speaking through me
Angelite, create from darkness

Angelite, Part 2

When can I see you again, my dear friend ?
I have not seen your smile in a while
Your face I can not forget
I have this one regret
I did not confide
I chose to hide
My deepest desire to
rekindle our flame
Do you feel the same ?
My strong feelings remain
I put your face in a frame with your name

Today was just another day
After I got off work
I went home to sit alone
No messages on the phone
There is no laughter
Nothing more after
The echoes of my sigh
The echoes of my cry
I regret this pain inside

The next morning I rise
To my surprise
I see your shining eyes
You are my day light
You make the dark clouds turn bright
No more room for gloom

My Angelite I need your warm touch

Angelique Kereecko

I miss you so much
This time I keep it real
Explain how I feel
I cherish our bond
I express my love
I care for you so much
We elevate together
We are more than friends
I hold you dear to my heart
We are stronger together
Do not think to grow apart
You encourage me
Help me to see the way that you see
You bring out the best in me

Angelique Kereecko

Loyal Twin Flames

I told you, I would never leave you
I told you, I walk with you through the fire
We crash and burn in the flame together
Your name is forever engraved in my brain
You believe the same

In the beginning we chose one another
There is no mistake about our union
This is loyal love, real in the flesh
We together into the death
We marry into this loyalty
Through heaven and hell, we do prevail
Through the rain and pain, we still remain
There is no maybe, this is definitely

Angelique Kereecko

Hypnotize and Mesmerize

Hypnotize and mesmerize with these thighs
Lock me into your eyesight
Fall further into paradise
This love is a blessing
Your touch is a blessing
Your kiss is a blessing
Forever and however we are together
Your body melt into mine
Our bodies intertwine
No need to speak
We have telepathy
We have unity
We have eternity
We create our love destiny
We create our love energy
We create our longevity

Your body is mine
My body is yours
Take me to the highest heights
Take flight through our minds
Take flight above the sky
We are not stopped by time

Angelique Kereecko

Love In The Air

I feel love in the air
I feel love everywhere
I smell love in the air
I smell love everywhere
I see love in the air
I see love everywhere
I taste love in the air
I taste love everywhere

You breathe into me
You give me life
I breathe into you
I give you life
Beautiful creatures
We are closer than close

Angelique Kereecko

In Love With Your Spirit

I pray to your spirit
I worship your spirit
I am devoted to your spirit
I am in love with your spirit
The essence of your presence is a blessing
We come together in the name of love spirit

Touch me
Hold me
Caress me
Console me
We complement one another
Our energy matches perfectly
We get high with our spirits
Appreciate your energy
Appreciate your telepathy
You know how to flow with me

Angelique Kereecko

Bed and Breakfast

Bed and breakfast is heavenly
I'm horny when I first wake up
Enjoy all this natural
Keep feeding me butter biscuits
Lick that Strawberry jelly off my fatty
Enjoy this breakfast baby
Eat every drop
Please don't stop

Bed and breakfast is heavenly
I'm hungry when I first wake up
Enjoy all this natural
Keep feeding me home-made pancakes
Pour that syrup on my kitty
Enjoy this breakfast baby
Drink every drop
Please don't stop

Drink milk from my breast
Quench your thirst

Angelique Kereecko

Beautiful Combination Creation

This is for the light skin
Race mixing is not a sin
Light skin had been existing since the beginning of time
The heart can not define who to love
Light skin we have always been here
Light skin we always remain here
Generation after generation
Century after century

I understand the Pro-Black mentality
You understand that us Bi-racials and Mixed Kins
need room to breath to simply be our unique selves
I do embrace my American Indigenous Cherokee
I am a different breed
I am something in between
Beautiful combination creation
The best of both worlds
Light skin was created for a beautiful purpose
American Indigenous
Kereecko is my identity

I have outgrown the "you not black enough" argument
As a child I heard this too many times
As an adult I still hear this in 2023
I accept, respect and love my Black Half
I choose to disconnect from the toxicity
In this 21st Century, I assumed that the Pro-Black Mentality
would be more progressive
I can not convert to this negativity
I still embrace the Black Positivity

Every second
Every minute

Angelique Kereecko

Every hour
Every day
Every month
Every year
We are still born
Living
Breathing
Populating

Thank You for listening
Thank You for no longer criticizing my existence

Angelique Kereecko

Sadness

I live sadness
I breathe sadness
I eat sadness
I sleep sadness
This lingering dark sadness

I don't know where it starts
I don't know where it ends
It's a never ending cycle
Am I the only 1 who feels like this ?

You attach to me like my Twin
You follow me like my Shadow
Where did You come from?
How did You find me ?
Do we ever part ways ?
I guess, I'm never alone

Angelique Kereecko

Wild Like A Wolf

I'm wild like a wolf
I'm untamed
Don't ask me to change
I got my own personality
I do whatever I want
You better accept all of me

If I'm too bold for you
Then move on
Don't waste your time
You keep trying to convince me
It is my delight to bite
I might not spare you
I do enjoy every chew

I'm in love with my wild energy
I can not be controlled
You can join me
But, don't try to change me
You better accept all of me

Angelique Kereecko

Thirsty, Horney Bull

You are the reflection of myself
Masculine and Feminine are intertwined,
Your essence is Divine

Your skin, your hair smells like Egyptian Musk
Your beard rubs gently in between my breast
Your lips softly caress my neck
Your firm chest muscles holds my head
Your strong arms are a gentle embrace
Your strong hands hold me tightly
Promise, never let me go

You are the reflection of myself
Masculine and Feminine are intertwined
Your essence is Divine

We kiss under the moonlight
Your lips feel softer than silk
Your black eyes shine bright
You stand tall and I am protected
Your body is a beautiful sculpture
Your tawny skin feels smooth
Your long black poppin' curls are perfection

You are the reflection of myself
Masculine and Feminine are intertwined
Your essence is Divine

Our Destiny is written in the Stars
There is no reason to wonder where you are

Angelique Kereecko

Your Soul and Spirit is never too far
We have met for our Divine appointment
Our Divine connection is unbreakable
We have this strong energy
That last into infinity

You are the reflection of myself
Masculine and Feminine are intertwined
Your essence is Divine

Angelique Kereecko

Sweet Divine

Sweet like sugar
Smooth like silk

Sweet like honey
Smooth like butter

Sweet like caramel
Smooth like lace

Sweet like the finest taste
Only in the exclusive place
Experience enchanting, enticing, inviting
You close enough to look
Still, you can not touch this Sweet Divine
My presence is like sweet fragrance
Feel my Holy Presence
I am all through this temple

Experience Sweet Sacredness
Admire Sweet Innocence
Worship Sweet Presence

Angelique Kereecko

You Wish

You see me in the flesh
You wish that you could see through me
You wish that you could read into me
You wish that you knew what I'm up to
You wish that you knew me well
So very well
You wish that you could keep me all to yourself
But, remember this
I am not to be kept
I am not a bird in a cage
I am that beautiful Divine Creature that you seek
I am the answer to your prayers
You summoned me from the depths of your mind
Finally, I do arrive
Our paths written in the Stars
We are no longer worlds apart
Can you spark the flame within my heart ?
Are we truly Divine Twin Flames ?
You wish that you could experience the depths of my love
You wish to reciprocate genuine love
No judgment
No harsh words spoken
No abusing
You wish that you had the key to my heart
I know and understand your desires
Do you deserve to see into me ?
You wish upon a Venus star

Angelique Kereecko

Dancing In The Sky

Let your power take you high
I can not deny
I love to go high
This moment is the highlight of your life

Dancing in the sky
Morning, noon and night
Starting in July
Travel through twilight

I can not deny
I love to go high
This is how I take flight

Angelique Kereecko

Poem To Self

Don't be afraid to upgrade
Don't be afraid to adjust to change
Don't be afraid to level up
Don't be afraid to grow up

Follow my shoes
Teach you the rules
Show you the moves

You can have a master plan
Hope you understand
I'm keeping it real
You understand what you feel
Do what you need to
Realize the greatness within you

Angelique Kereecko

My Dear Love

My Dear Love, I wait patiently for you
I have high hopes to meet you
My heart is over excited to be in love with you
I want to meet you wherever you are
We can meet on planet Earth
We can meet in another dimension,
in another place and time
We can meet in another galaxy
Will I meet you in this life time or in the next ?

My Dear Love, I have prepared a place in my heart for you
I have prepared my house for you
I have prepared room in my life for you

My Dear Love, our kindred spirits unite in the perfect timing
We build our empire together
We endure through whatever
Your business combined with my creativity is the perfect recipe that we need
Your masculine and my feminine is the perfect combination
In Love Forever and
Forever In Love

Angelique Kereecko

Better Than Yesterday

Today is better than yesterday
Obstacles moved out my way
I'm living the best of my life
I got my good spell
I'm walking in my blessings

Dear Self, you deserve the very best
These blessings are on my life
I'm walking in my blessings
I'm living in my blessings

I see myself with a brighter future
You are doing well
You got good health
You got good wealth

Angelique Kereecko

Swim

Swim deep in love
Making love all night
Keep holding me tight
My eyes are heavy sleepy
Each kiss keeps me awake
How much my body can take
I never get enough
Making love into the morning
is the greatest feeling
We never tell each other No

You open wide
Let it flow into you
I open wide
Let it flow into me
Dive deep
Don't stop
Swim deep
Don't stop
Explore all of me
Don't stop

We go to Wet Land
We swim together at the same pace
You love to dive deep into my ocean
I love drinking from your fountain
You swim in my ocean of love
I am the Mermaid
You are the Explorer
I'm the greatest gem you have ever found
My love is worth more than silver and gold

Angelique Kereecko

My world is the greatest that you have ever known

You open wide
Let it flow into you
I open wide
Let it flow into me
Dive deep
Don't stop
Swim deep
Don't stop
Explore all of me
Don't stop

Welcome to the Holy Fountain of Love
Drink my Holy water
I promise that
You never thirst anymore
My Holy water keeps flowing
day after day
Bless your lips with my Holy water
Bless you with love from my thighs
Taste, Drink, Swallow my Holy water

You open wide
Let it flow into you
I open wide
Let it flow into me
Dive deep
Don't stop
Swim deep
Don't stop
Explore all of me
Don't stop

Angelique Kereecko

Touch Your Flesh

I grabbed through your picture, touch your flesh
Finally, you here with me
Where you need to be
Do you realize this?
It is a most definitely
No more fantasy
It is a reality
No more dreaming
Do you realize this?
My wish has come true
Touchable
Enjoyable
Excitable
Your sweetness is delicious
There is no other like your essence
I need your caress as we undress
Naked in your presence is a blessing
Oh, yes it is
With every glance, we fall deeper into each other's eyes

Hypnotize and mesmerize with these thighs
Lock me into your eye sight
Fall further into paradise
This love is a blessing
Your touch is a blessing
Your kiss is a blessing
Forever, however we are together

Your body melt into mine
Our bodies intertwine
No need to speak
We have telepathy
We have unity

Angelique Kereecko

We have eternity
We create our love destiny
We create our love energy
We create our longevity

You body is mine
My body is yours
Take me to the highest heights
Take flight through our minds
Take flight above the sky
We are not stopped by time

Angelique Kereecko

Emotionally Broken

Heart is broken
Emotions broken
Will to move on is broken
Motivation is foreign to conceive
Determination is foreign to see
No hope to believe
Calling for an Angel
Dear God send me an Angel

I'm in the lowest depths
It's all darkness, no hope left
This heart is shredded
This heart torn into a million pieces
Calling for an Angel
Dear God send me an Angel

Bless me with wings to soar
Let the sunshine in
These eyes need to see the light
I need an Angel to lift me high
Lift me with your wings
My Angel, help me experience
blissful things
To the heavenly Angel, I sing
Calling for an Angel
Dear God send me an Angel

Angelique Kereecko

We Persevere

Didn't I tell you, that I am here for you
Didn't I tell you, that I am here with you
Look how far we've come
I am still here on this journey with you
Through the rain
Through the storm
Through the pain
Our plans are clear
We are too sincere
No doubt interfere
We are a power couple
We build our empire
Through the fears and tears
we made it here
Finally, we are featured
in our own premiere
Yes Dear, we say a cheer
under the chandelier

Angelique Kereecko

Cake and Bake

When I get my new wig
I wear the hell out of it
Lookn good
Lookn snatched
Slayn makeup
My banana powder bake for that cake face
My foundation ain't going no where
My cut-crease eyeshadow is waterproof
My glitter makeup glistening to the glam Gods
My lipstick stuck on pretty all day
My luscious lashes lovely
I got that glam glow
Let my soul glow
This highlight glow to the Gods
My face is sculpted
My contour is flawless
Cake and bake
Cake, bake, slay
Cake and bake
Cake, bake, slay
Money and makeup go hand in hand
Both are a girls' best friend

Angelique Kereecko

Empath

I give all that I could
You know that I care
I give more than I should
You know that I be there
I give you love to heal your Soul
My love is your Salvation
I been strong for the both of us
When I need a Saviour,
Can you be strong for the both of us ?
Can you be strong times two ?
Can you be strong like I do ?

Remember every time I promise you
Remember every time I follow through
Remember every time I pull through
Remember every time I'm there with you
I am true through and through

I heal your broken heart
So we don't fall apart
Always see the best in you
Always believe in you
Always encourage you
I give you love to heal your Soul
My love is your Salvation
I been strong for the both of us
When I need a Saviour,
Can you be strong for the both of us ?
Can you be strong times two ?
Can you be strong like I do ?

Remember every time I promise you
Remember every time I follow through

Angelique Kereecko

Remember every time I pull through
Remember every time I'm there with you
I am true through and through

I pour so much into you
I'm surprised that I have something
left for myself
I give so you can make it too
I'm by your side day and night
With me, everything is alright
I bless you
I console you
I comfort you
My compassion is the truth

Angelique Kereecko

Sweeter Than Honey

You like to taste the finer things in life
You like fancy
You search for the very best
You like luxury
You crave that sweet honey drip
You smell that sweet honey drip
You anxious to taste that sweeter than honey

When you look in the right place at the right time
This sweet treasure you can find
Experience pleasure without measure
Imagine, be with me, infinity
Love you to the moon and back
Love you beyond climax
Our bodies intertwine
You are forever mine
1,000 degrees hot in heat
Sweat flow, temperature rise
Juices flow, temperature rise high
Honey drip flow, temperature rise higher

I'm sweeter than honey
Come to me
I'll be all you need

Lick, drink, taste delicious, honeyilicious
Kisses taste sweeter than honey
Tongue soft like silk

Lick, drink, taste delicious, honeyilicious
Breasts taste sweeter than honey
Nipples soft like silk

Angelique Kereecko

Lick, drink, taste delicious, honeyilicious
Kitty taste sweeter than honey
Clit soft like silk

Lick, drink, taste delicious, honilicious
Booty juice taste sweeter than honey
Booty soft like silk

Lick, drink, taste delicious, honilicious
Sweeter than honey

Angelique Kereecko

Pretty Confidence

Fine, fit, curvy
Light skin with long hair
People stop and stare
But, I don't care
Admire my beauty
Naturally pretty
My energy glowin' and shinin'
Confident in my skin
Beautiful within
Long hair frame my face
Bouncy curls blowin' in the wind
I'm in love with all my beauty
Naturally pretty that's just how I be
Ain't got no flaws
In my eyes, I am Divine
I am perfectly pretty
No time for envy
The enemy is beneath me
Light skin always exist
Realize this
Accept it and move on
Have pretty confidence in your light skin
Light skin is not a trend
Embrace your beauty from within
My name is not mulatto
My name is not redbone
My name is not mixie
My name name is not yellow bone
My anime is not bougie
My name is indigenous
My name is Kereecko
Cherokee is my Family
I am dedicated to my family roots

Angelique Kereecko

Big Booty, Wow !

Pretty, Plump, Perfect
Big, Smooth, Round
Shake up and down
Both cakes weigh 10 pounds
Shake the left cake
Shake the right cake
Pour the whip cream
Lick that booty clean
Such a good feelin'
I'm livin' my dream
Big booty bounce
Both cakes weigh 10 pounds
Love to lick that booty
Cocktail glass on that ass
Mass ass worship
Take a trip into ass worship
Slippery slip ass worship
Fucking freaky relationship ass worship
Naked strip, money tip, ass worship
Penis double dip, ass worship
Smell fresh like a tulip, ass worship
Don't be late to the queenship
Enjoy ass worship
Lip serving ass worship
Enter into the goddessship
In love with ass worship
Have no guilt trip for this ass worship
Put that hot tip dick in this ass worship
Go deep until your knees get weak
Lip drip pussywhip
Lip drip pussywhip
Lip drip pussywhip
You go balls deep, put me to sleep

Angelique Kereecko

I like this devils' grip with ass worship
Taste that booty drip, ass worship
Taste that booty drip, ass worship
Taste that booty drip, ass worship
Smother your face in this booty
Hug this booty
Make love to this booty
Taste that booty drip, ass worship

Angelique Kereecko

Love Letter To Myself

Dear Divine Body,
I appreciate You
I worship You
I care for You
I adore You
I am in love with You
Beautiful Divine Body
Beautiful Divine Goddess

I love the way You move
Smooth like poetry
I love the way You smell
fresh after bathing
I love Your bouncy curly hair
I love Your perfectly shaped face
I love Your nipples on Your warm full breasts
Beautiful Divine Body
Beautiful Divine Goddess

I love Your natural curves
I gently put my finger tips on Your hips
I love the size of Your thick thighs
I love the smell of Your plump precious pussy
I love the feel of Your soft sexy derrière
Pretty precious peach
Fresh and juicy
Beautiful Divine Body
Beautiful Divine Goddess

I love to feel Your wide calves
I love to massage Your feet
I sit in front of the mirror
Open, open, open wide

Angelique Kereecko

I see ALL the greatest wonders inside
No one is greater than I
I am luxury
Beautiful Divine Body
Beautiful Divine Goddess

Angelique Kereecko

Dear Sweet Darling

Oh, I'm missing your pretty smile
It's been a while since the last I seen you
I got used to you always being there
Every morning and night
Every morning I wake up to your Angel face
I feel your warm embrace
I wanted you to be mine everyday
Oh, tell me, why you went away
As I think things over
I can not help but wonder
What can I do to get you back ?
I remember our sweet time
Your hands in mine
Dear God, can I press rewind ?
I looked for you high and low
Where did you go ?
I looked here and there and everywhere
I can not find you anywhere

The last time we talked you said
You wanted more quality time
I'm willing to do that
You got to be mine
Deep down in my soul, I believe you
and I are meant to be
I be your Mrs. Forever
You my Mr. Forever
We stay together to make it through whatever
I appreciate all the good things you do
Your love is more than enough
I miss cookin' for you
I miss talkin' to you
I miss holdin' you

Angelique Kereecko

I miss lovin' you
Come back, sweet darlin'
I do cherish you
I do need you
You're the only one who can make it right

Dear God, bless us to cross paths
Rekindle the passion
We deserve to be in love
Angels in Heaven, please answer my prayers
Any day I'm expecting to see your Angel face
As I was sitting in the park
There you are walking my way
My heart is filled with joy
to see your smiling face
Dark clouds suddenly disappear
as you walk near
As we talk things over
We understand each other much better
We both love each other just the same
Thank God, we rekindle our flame
No more searching for true love
Months later the wedding bells are ringing
We are singing our heavenly love
Sweet darling you were sent from above

Angelique Kereecko

Wind Song

I hear the wind whisper
I hear the wind whistling
I see the wind flow
I feel the wind blow
This is natures' song
carries the voice of the birds
Sweet sounds I have heard
Wind guiding me through the galaxy
Wind carry me through the stargate
Meet my Creator face to face
Creator calling above the clouds
I am not Earth bound
I travel beyond the cloud
The sky is endless
My journey is fearless
Higher, higher
I feel the wind blow
I see the wind flow
I hear the wind whistling
I hear the wind whisper

Angelique Kereecko

I Have To Go/ What If

I cared too much
I gave too much
I did love too much
This is enough
You never reciprocated
This is the end of us
I must say good-bye
for the last time
I can not wipe the
tears from your eyes
I can not listen
to you cry

I turn around
Can not slow down
No reminisce on the past
Can not look back
No longer desire what we had
I must face the facts
No reason to be sad

What if we never said good-bye
What if you never made me cry
What if you became more serious
What if you help to grow our love
What if you help me to trust

What if you reciprocate the way that I do
What if you officially marry me
I would like to give so much more
I would like to give all my love
I would not hesitate to make
you the center of my attention

Angelique Kereecko

I would not hesitate to
give you all my affection
Promise to you baby
there is no rejection
You would be my Husband
My 1 and only Husband

Angelique Kereecko

The Beauty of Silence

Focus your thoughts
Obsess with your thoughts
Focus on your thoughts
Learn this lesson
Focus on your obsession
Show your progression
Look within
Create the world you want to live in

What plan did you create ?
What action did you take ?
What progress did you make ?
No excuse for mental escape
No excuse to sit and wait
All the answers you find inside your mind
Be self-taught with your thought
Let your thought nourish your vision
Let your thought give fire to your desire
Realize your mind is a gold mine

Angelique Kereecko

High Gods

I am your creation
Your agenda carries through
every generation
Your Holy Names deserve veneration
I worship your presence
I respect your intelligence
I admire your essence
You are Divine by your own design
From high above the sky
I spend time with you
I am grateful for every moment
Take the time to talk
The knowledge and secrets I do cherish
I keep these things safe within my heart
In this life time
I go high
Elevate beyond the sky

Angelique Kereecko

Try

I kept my promise to you
I need you to keep yours, too
Not maybe
I need
Yes definitely
Do it faithfully just like me
Am I the only one being responsible ?
This isn't fair
Don't expect me to care
Can you try to meet me half way there ?
All I wanted was the best for us
I guess something is wrong with me
Now, I must clearly see
We are not compatibility
Can you try to keep our love alive ?
Do you want to be dead weight ?
You don't answer
I no longer wait

Angelique Kereecko

Conversations In The Grave

I see you as clear as day
Your spirit talks
You're not dead
Your spirit walks
You're not dead
Your words feel cold like the wind
I listen about your soul journey
I am thankful that you chose me
I am the vessel that you need
Your energy is still alive
You're not dead
Your spirit is still alive
You're not dead
Your photos captured your memory in time
Your energy is infinite
Your energy is alive
Yes, of course I remember you
Your soul is unforgettable

Angelique Kereecko

I Do

I do accept all of you
The light and the darkness within you

I do accept your angel
I do accept your demon

I do accept your good
I do accept your bad

I do accept your happiness
I do accept your sadness

I do accept your strength
I do accept your weakness

I do accept your joy
I do accept your pain

I do accept your laughter
I do accept your tears

I do accept your bravery
I do accept your fears

I do accept you in the brightest light
I do accept you in the darkness of the night

Angelique Kereecko

Nosey Bitch

I'm

Anti-social

Quiet

Silent

Introvert

I can't stan a nosey bitch

Asking 100 questions

And the main 1 snitchin'

I don't say shit

I move in silence

Ask me somethin'

I be honest

I say "No comment"

These dudes be nosey bitches, too

Talkn smooth pretending he care

He want to know my plans

I ain't telling the real real 'bout what I do

I'm

Anti-social

Quiet

Silent

Introvert

Where did she go ?

You don't know

Invisible, real quick get ghost

That's okay

No bring tag-a-long

Nosey bitches don't belong

You feel too comfortable tryn' to probe

You want to get too close

Stay out my zone

This is my world

Can't relate to me

Angelique Kereecko

Fuck your curiosity
I'm
Anti-social
Quiet
Silent
Introvert

Bitches be nosey as hell
They be askin'
How much money ya makin' ?
Their money is nothin'.
They be askin'
How much money ya countin' ?
Their money is nothin'.
They be askin'
What's ya money flow ?
Their money is zero.
Ya bank account filled with zero's
Ya pockets on empty with a capital E
Tell me somethin'
Why ya wanna know about mine ?
Go somewhere else to get ya next meal
I swear nosey mother fuckers get on my nerves
I'm
Anti-social
Quiet
Silent
Introvert

Angelique Kereecko

Into The Afterlife

When I die, I join you in the afterlife
I still keep my promise to you
I love you yesterday
I love you today
I love you tomorrow
My love for you remains faithful and true
You are forever my twin flame
Our hearts never fall apart
As the roses bloom
My love for you
Grows stronger each day

When it's my time, I will be happy, to join you in the afterlife
No more tears
No more fears
No more weary
No more worry
No more pain
No more strain

You still have my love and loyalty, forever, into the afterlife
I lived my life to the fullest
I have no regrets
I gave love
I received love
We created our best moments
We created our best secrets
We created our best love
You washed away my sadness with your happiness

Angelique Kereecko

Not Forgotten

Our memories are never lost in time
I replay precious memories in my head until we reunite
I never lose track of time
I count the days until we embrace again
In the recess of my mind
I press rewind
I relive the greatest times in our lives
I believe we will meet again
I miss your smile
Your laughter echoes in my mind
These precious memories never fade away
You are confined in that hell jail cell
You are not forgotten

Angelique Kereecko

Lovely Venus

Hour after hour
We make love
In the shower
Your body is calling
Your dick is craving
I am right where you need me to be
I am surrounded by your love
I am wrapped up in your love
I am baptized in your love
This is beyond imagination
Experience the sweetest temptation
On the highest elevation
In the constellation
We are stars creating
We travel through each other's mind
We take flight beyond the sky

Angelique Kereecko

I See The Good In You - Part 1
I don't believe it
I can not believe it
This is someone different
than I know you to be
I know who you are to me
I hear the bad things people say about you
Regardless, I am still true to you
I know who you are to me
I see the good in you
This is all I know to see
Am I wearing rose glasses ?
Maybe or maybe not
Either way
I see the good in you
This is all I know to see

In this cruel world
We are each others' anchor
We lift each other up
We build our own heaven
We build our happy home
We create our peace of mind
Just you and me
All I need to see
Is the good that you show me

You are good enough for me
I just see the very best in you
We give the best of ourselves to one another
In this cruel world, I choose to hold onto you
I choose to see the good in you
Promise, not to break my heart into two
Keep giving me every reason to stay
I love to be in love this way

Angelique Kereecko

I See The Good In You – Part 2
I only see the best in you
I only want what is the best for you
I want to grow with you
I want to celebrate with you
I want to create with you
Create good times with you
is all I want to do
I know who you are to me
I see the good in you
This is all I know to see
Am I wearing rose glasses ?
Maybe or maybe not
Either way
I see the good in you
This is all I know to see

I don't know another way to be
I see roses through my glasses
I see your happiness
This means the world to me

I like to bring a good balance
Is this your challenge ?
Are you ready for a higher level ?
I only go up
Are you ready for a new level ?
Take my hand, have no fear
on this new journey
I choose to see the good in you
Promise, not to break my heart into two
Keep giving me every reason to stay
I love to be in love this way

Angelique Kereecko

Away To Her Planet

He says: Woman, where you going ?

She says: To Planet Venus

He says: Can I come with you ?

She says: No men allowed

He says: Why not ?

She says: This is private entry
Don't envy me
Here, I have a new beginning
I deserve this opportunity
I break away from toxic patriarchy
I choose to embrace the positive matriarchy
I choose to align to the Goddess within me
I am happy that my mind is free

Angelique Kereecko

I Want To . . .
I just want to get to know you
Yeah, yeah, yeah
We can sit and talk
Discover each other
Uncover your feelings
Explore mentality
Explore energy
Explore spirituality
Explore quality
Explore possibility for compatibility

I'm excited to get to know you
I hope you are curious the same
You are more than your name
I'm looking for my twin flame

I can see inside your heart
I am careful with your heart
I am patient with your heart
No more wishing on a star
We have made it this far
We can go beyond the stars
Combine our time
Combine our minds
Become one mind
Forever intertwined
No more fantasy
We build our reality
Lovers hand in hand

I really would like to know you
Life is precious
I cherish every waking moment

Angelique Kereecko

I cherish every beat of your heart
I cherish every breath you take
I cherish the sound of your voice
I cherish the vibrations of your tone
I appreciate to share your journey as your life blossoms
I celebrate the most profound moments with you

Angelique Kereecko

Your Vibe

I been searching for you all my life
I'm in love with your vibe
I finally found someone who
deserves to be in my life
Finally found my special someone
You are perfectly compatible to me
Your energy is lovely
Your energy is perfectly compatibility

Your smile brightens my day
Your laughter is the highlight
Your joy is the best of my day
Your eyes bring sunshine to my life

I cherish every breath you take
I cherish the sound of your voice
I cherish the vibrations of your tone
I appreciate to share your journey as your life blossoms
I celebrate the most profound moments with you

Your love is what I live for
Each day I pray for you to stay
forever and always
Please promise, we are together for a life time
I do anything to keep you in my life

Angelique Kereecko

Darkness

I am in love with the darkness
I respect the darkness
I do not dare play with this
I am attracted to this
I am pulled into this
I follow my soul
I live in this darkness
I thrive in darkness
I am my happiest
I live my best in darkness
I am loyal to the darkness
I am committed to my Dark Goddess

Angelique Kereecko

In Love With All of Myself

I am in love with all of me
My light, my dark
My good, my bad
My angel, my demon

I am not crazy
I am being real
Keep your criticism to yourself
Fuck your small opinion
I just love being myself

Living out loud no apology
I prosper in the light with my Angel
I manifest in the darkness with my Demon
I am living my truth
My action is proof

I accept my reflection in the mirror
I embrace all my Energy
I am not shy
I do not hide

Angelique Kereecko

Poem From The Dark

I put my pain on display
I am not afraid
I am not ashamed
You know my name
This is how I became

Through the years I do change
Do my best to heal my pain
I can not change the beginning of my life
I can not change my birth date
But, I can change how I heal
I choose to empower myself
I have learned to love who I am
I accept the Goddess who I have become

I walk with my Shadow
My Shadow is my best friend
I am in love with my own darkness
I found my best self in the Shadow
I am in love with myself
I am in love with my own darkness
I found my best self in the Shadow
I found my liberation
Finally, I deliver myself into my Ascension

Angelique Kereecko

Your Healing Touch

Each time you touch me
I get a good feeling
Your touch is my healing
Your fingertips caress my hips
I love it
You touch me slowly
You touch me gently
I feel you
I taste you on my lips
Your energy surrounds me
I'm wrapped up in your light
This I do not fight
There is no fear or flight
You make love to my soul
I love it
I submit to your control
You complete me
Promise to keep me
Just love me
Don't deplete me

Angelique Kereecko

Magickal Nite

We are living this moment
hear and now
We are strong together
We are better together
We hold onto each other
We found each other in darkness
You light the spark in my heart
I am your Queen
You are my King
We rule with clarity
We create prosperity
We found goodness in our darkness
We found love in the darkness
I must confess
I love you at your worst
I love you at your best

Angelique Kereecko

Listen To Your Soul
Dear Beautiful Soul
I listen to your Soul
I hear your silent cries
I feel your heartbeat in the darkness
I feel your dark pain
I see your struggle
My empathy is strong for the both of us

Dear Beautiful Soul
Please take a moment
Look within yourself
Visualize yourself doing better
Let your Soul heal
Smile, get happy from within
Imagine all the positive possibilities
See yourself taking that first step to a new chapter
You look and feel better in the here and after

Dear Beautiful Soul
Focus on your vision
Start your mission
Let yourself enjoy life on this new level
Believe you deserve to have better
Hope my compassion is the water that you need
Hope my encouragement is the light that you need
Hope my positivity is the vibe that you need
I listen to Your Soul

Sincerely,

Lady Angelique

Angelique Kereecko

Happy Summer Dayz
Family picnics
Blowing bubbles
Playin' on the water slide
Enjoy the fun ride
Happy for the summer
120 degrees no cool breeze
Popsicles are sweet relief
Bom popsicles are the best treat

Wearin' tank tops
Wearin' crocs
Dancin' in the street
Pop lock drop it
Move to the beat
Pop lock drop it
Move your feet
Pop lock drop it
Dancin' to the beat

Lookin' pretty
Makeup on fleek
Big booty small waist
Slayin' my neon cut crease
Pretty smilin'
Wearing neon lipstick
Warm sun caress my skin
Pool party begin
Dancin' and eatin' wit my friends
We party from sunrise 'til night

Angelique Kereecko

Dear Shadow

Hello Shadow, I never let You go
Dear Shadow, You are dark and beautiful
You feed my soul to survive

Dear Shadow, I love You
when I'm young

Dear Shadow, I love You
When I'm old

Dear Shadow, You are apart of me
together for eternity
I am never ashamed of thee

Dear Shadow, You are there through thick and thin
You are my best friend

Dear Shadow, I am in love with You

Dear Shadow, You are my precious
I cherish You

Angelique Kereecko

Peace

Like the peace and quiet
Shut the world out
Cancel my instagram
Turn my phone off
Listen to the waterfalls
Gives me relief
Enjoy my inner peace
I ain't missing anything in this world
Connect to my spiritual
Fly to a higher level
Astral travel
Ain't missing planet Earth
Nah, nah, never
Comfortable above the clouds
Go to another dimension is my intention

Angelique Kereecko

Sacred Rose

I love the way your Aura glows
You are my Sacred Rose
You belong to the cosmos
You bring Heaven to Earth
Your love so addictive I overdose
The first sight of You makes me propose
Tight bond between us
Our secrets we do not disclose
Our circle we do enclose
Each kiss from You melts my heart
This heart no longer froze
Your love is my healing
You know my diagnose
Our most precious moments are grandiose

Angelique Kereecko

I Would Rather

I would rather be a glistening star seed

I would rather that I descend from planet Venus
bringing my Goddess energy
than waiting for a saviour to rescue me

I would rather be a glamorous creatress
launching glitter rockets into the world
than waiting for the next inventor to manifest

The function of my Queenship is amazingly great and awesome
according to my standards

I would rather combine my time with the man who makes a firm decision

I would rather dive deep into my ocean of abundance

I would rather flow into my prosperity

I would rather flow with my prosperity

Angelique Kereecko

Deep Down Under

In my deep down under
Deeply rooted in it
Something good comes from it
My little seed grows tall and mighty
Don't overlook the beginning
Eyes wide open
Pay close attention
I mention you need to listen
Pressed to perfection in the process
I am like a diamond under pressure
You wonder what I'm planning
You wonder how I'm moving
You wonder what I'm doing
You probing with your questions
You comfortable being nosey
You wonder why I hide in darkness
You wonder why I move in silence
I tell you this one secret
I rather hide from your spying eyes
Be patient
You see the greatness
My progress looks like a surprise

Angelique Kereecko

Dear Ancestors

Dear Ancestors you paved the way
for me to be great
You gave me the key to succeed
I am Thankful for all you've done
Every sacrifice you made
You did more than enough
Confident like the sun rays
Brave like a million lions
You did more than roar
You fought war after war
Elders encourage me
I honour your victories

Tsitsalagi

Angelique Kereecko

Healing Heart

I care deep enough for you
Let my love be your anchor
My love for you is deeper than the ocean
Feel this deep vibration
Feel this deep emotion
I'm your saviour
Angel wings catch you before you fall
I can not help but to give you life
My energy is your oxygen
Our love grows to full bloom
Sunshine surrounding you
Loving you is my special occasion

No wall is too tall to reach you
No gate is too strong to reach you
No bridge is too wide to reach you
No road is too long to reach you
My love is pure and unconditional
My love is your medicine
healing your broken heart

Angelique Kereecko

Love Notes

These love notes are the songs of the heart
Your Venus pulls at my heart strings
But don't dare play with my emotions
Angels fill the air with harmonies and melodies
I'm wrapped up in this love
I'm caught up in this love
I'm tied up in this love

Play this love story with the harp
I give to you my heart
Play this love story with the violin
Our unity does begin
Play this love story with the cello
Our love does grow

With Libra in Venus we have balance
As the orchestra plays in the background
The angels sing harmonies and melodies
Our love grows in our favor
We created this glorious love
We are deeply rooted in this glorious love
We are glorious, glorious, glorious

Play this love story with the harp
I give to you my heart
Play this love story with the violin
Our unity does begin
Play this love story with the cello
Our love does grow

Baby match my tone in this frequency
Sing with this melody
Baby put your body in tune with mine

Angelique Kereecko

Celebrate our glorious love
We discover one another
Give and receive pleasure without measure
Our love making is like a sweet ballad that never ends, never, never, never

Play this love story with the harp
I give to you my heart
Play this love story with the violin
Our unity does begin
Play this love story with the cello
Our love does grow

Hear these love notes calling your name
Accept it, Receive it, Appreciate it, Believe it

Angelique Kereecko

Flow

I flow just like the wind
You don't know how I flow
You don't know where I come
You don't know where I go
You don't know where I begin
You don't know where I end
You don't know how I flow
I am invisible just like the wind
You don't know where I begin
You don't know where I end
I am uncontrollable just like the wind
You can not hold onto me
You can not catch me
Like the wind, I move swiftly
I flow like the wind
Flow like the wind

Angelique Kereecko

Spiritual Love

Our love grows stronger everyday
I love you in a special way
Oh, sweet heart don't let those haters tear us apart
We made our decision
We have no division
Our love is our religion
We dedicated to our mission
We loyal to the death
We faithful now and in the afterlife

We have a strong bond
From my heart to yours
Our love brings us together
You are the fire to my flame
Darling, remember our vision
Focus on our mission

In each life time, we still unite
In each life time, you are mine
We are forever twin flames
Never forget your name
Never forget your face
Our strong bond remain the same

We have a strong bond
From my heart to yours
Our love brings us together
You are the fire to my flame
Darling, remember our vision
Focus on our mission

In my mind, I press rewind
I replay memories of you and I

Angelique Kereecko

Beautiful Souls Let's Connect !

Official Website@ AngeliqueKereecko.com

Poetry Planet Podcast @ https://angelique-kereecko.captivate.fm

My Art Work Portfolio @ http://dribbble.com/AngeliqueKereecko.com

The 1 and Only Social Media Profile @ http://instagram.com/AngeliqueKereeckoOfficial

Join Conversations @ https://www.threads.net/@angeliquekereeckoofficial

Exclusively For Members ONLY @ https://angelique-kereecko.captivate.fm/support

Heart of Passion © 2023